I0005690

HÄNSEL AND GRETEL

A GUIDE TO
ENGELBERT HUMPERDINCK'S
OPERA

BY

LEWIS M. ISAACS AND KURT J. RAHLSON

AUTHORS OF "A GUIDE TO KÖNIGSKINDER"

Frontispiece

NEW YORK

DODD, MEAD AND COMPANY

1913

Lewis M. Isaacs and
Kurt J. Rahlson:

Hänsel and Gretel
A Guide to Engelbert Humperdinck's Opera.

First published by Dodd, Mead & Co 1913.

Republished Travis & Emery 2009.

Published by
Travis & Emery Music Bookshop
17 Cecil Court, London, WC2N 4EZ, United Kingdom.
(+44) 20 7240 2129
neworders@travis-and-emery.com

Hardback: ISBN10: 1-906857-35-0   ISBN13: 978-1-906857-35-6
Paperback: ISBN10: 1-906857-36-9   ISBN13: 978-1-906857-36-3

Engelbert Humperdinck (1854-1921). German composer.

He attended Cologne Conservatory (1872-1876) and the Royal Music School in Munich.. He later worked with Wagner in Bayreuth.

His famous works are Hänsel und Gretel (1893), Königskinder (1897) and incidental music for four Shakespeare plays (1907-1908).

More details available from
- Stanley Sadie: The New Grove Dictionary of Music and Musicians.
- http://en.wikipedia.org/wiki/Humperdinck

Very little biographical information available in English.

Travis & Emery are republishing two works by Lewis M. Isaacs and Kurt J. Rahlson - Hänsel and Gretel: A Guide to Humperdinck's Opera and Königskinder (Royal Children): A Guide to Humperdinck's Opera.

© Travis & Emery 2009.

HÄNSEL AND GRETEL

BY THE SAME AUTHORS

KÖNIGSKINDER: A Guide to Engelbert
Humperdinck's and Ernst Rosmer's Opera

Drawing by T. Sindelar

Courtesy of The Legal Aid Society

HÄNSEL AND GRETEL

A GUIDE TO
ENGELBERT HUMPERDINCK'S
OPERA

BY

LEWIS M. ISAACS AND KURT J. RAHLSON

AUTHORS OF "A GUIDE TO KÖNIGSKINDER"

Frontispiece

NEW YORK
DODD, MEAD AND COMPANY
1913

COPYRIGHT, 1913
BY
DODD, MEAD AND COMPANY

Published, October, 1913

To

E. J. R. I.

PREFACE

As seems so often to be the case with masterpieces of art, the genesis of Hänsel and Gretel was purely fortuitous. Humperdinck's sister, Frau Adelheid Wette, arranged a little Christmas play for her children and asked the composer to set one of the scenes to music, which he did. This was the scene in what is now the first act of the opera, beginning with Gretel's invitation: "Brother, come and dance with me" (Brüderchen, komm tanz mit mir). Humperdinck became so interested in the possibilities for operatic treatment which the story held out, that he induced Frau Wette to make the play over into a libretto; and as it took shape it rapidly outgrew the original plan for a simple operetta suitable for amateur use. Under the direction of Richard Strauss it was first produced in Weimar in 1893. Soon every opera house in Germany was giving the work, and its popularity spread like wild-fire all over Europe. The first performance in America took place at Daly's Theatre in New York in October, 1895, under the direction of Anton Seidl. Ten years later it was taken over into the repertory of the Metropolitan Opera House and has remained there ever since, one of the favourite operas of young and old alike.

Twenty years have not dimmed its freshness, and constantly a new audience is being recruited from rising generations; so that the publication of a Guide to the opera seems justified even at this late day. The musical illustrations are intended to serve as finger-posts, while the translations from the original text, especially made for this book, will, it is hoped, also aid those who are not familiar with German to follow the performance more intelligently. For the particulars of Humperdinck's life, the reader is referred to the Preface of the "Königskinder" Guide, the cordial reception of which has encouraged the authors to make this attempt to enlarge still further the circle of the friends of the composer.

New York, September, 1913.

LEWIS M. ISAACS,
KURT J. RAHLSON.

TABLE OF CONTENTS

CAST OF CHARACTERS IN FIRST PERFORMANCE IN
AMERICA OF

HÄNSEL AND GRETEL

(Daly's Theatre, New York City, October 8, 1895)

PETER..........................*Jacques Bars*
GERTRUDE......................*Alice Gordon*
HÄNSEL........................*Marie Elba*
GRETEL ....*Jeanne Douste*
THE WITCH...............*Louise Meisslinger*
SANDMAN.......................*Cecile Brani*
DEWMAN.....................*Edith Johnston*

CONDUCTOR, Anton Seidl

CAST OF CHARACTERS IN FIRST PERFORMANCE AT
METROPOLITAN OPERA HOUSE OF

HÄNSEL AND GRETEL

(November 25, 1905)

HÄNSEL......................*Lina Abarbanell*
GRETEL.........................*Bella Alten*
GERTRUDE......................*Marion Weed*
THE WITCH...................*Louise Homer*
SANDMAN........................*Miss Moran*
DEWMAN.....................*Miss Glanville*
PETER...........................*Otto Goritz*

CONDUCTOR, Alfred Hertz

PART I

THE STORY

HÄNSEL AND GRETEL

"Exceeding rich and long and wide
And sprinkled with a sweet variety
Of all that pleasant is to the ear or eye"—

SUCH is the field of folklore. Folklore! The word
itself carries with it such whisperings of the hoarded
wisdom of the common people that it is with something of a shock one discovers it to be quite a modern
term, invented by Mr. W. J. Thoms, an English
littérateur, about the middle of the last century. But
though the word itself is young, the thing it desig-
nates does, indeed, take us back to the earliest begin-
nings of civilisation, to the infancy of the human
race.

For these tales of witches and fairies, of were-
wolves and enchanted princes, of cruel stepmothers
and maidens in distress, which have enthralled generation after generation, from dimmest antiquity
down to the present day, are the immediate result of
the first and all-unconscious impulse of the human
mind to cast into an artistic form, by means of the
story, the beliefs, superstitions and experiences ac-
quired from primitive man. They express, in short,
the primitive conception of the forces that made and
that rule the universe, just as the rude carvings on the

bones of an animal found in some prehistoric graves represent its expression in the form of handicraft.

These tales which, of course, originally made their appeal to the adult mind, gradually became the stock-in-trade of professional tale-bearers, who would relate them for the diversion of some Oriental monarch idling amid the splendors of his palace, or to beguile the slow hours of the long winter evenings at the blazing hearth-fire of some great hall in the North Countries. So, even in our own day, the recital by the priest or story-teller of weird and fabulous tales, no less fascinating because they are thoroughly familiar, remains a favourite pastime among savage or half-civilised tribes.

But as civilisation progressed to the point where the laws of nature were not all miracles to man, and the conditions underlying these tales were gradually outgrown, they were more and more used for the purpose of amusing or frightening children. With the little ones gathered around them, clamouring for a story, mothers and grandmothers would recollect and repeat the stories with which they themselves had been amused or frightened when they were young; and by that process these stories, adapted from time to time to new conditions of life, or embellished to allow for the particularly powerful imagination of some individual narrator, but unaltered in every essential part, were handed down through the ages and survived centuries that saw nearly every other heritage of the past crumble and disappear.

While we know of some collections of folk-tales (chiefly with a religious significance) made as far back as the seventeenth century, the scientific treatment of folk-lore is a comparatively recent achievement, having its inception in the work done by the Brothers Grimm at the beginning of the nineteenth century. Their collection of "Kinder und Hausmärchen" was gathered in a diligent search extending over a period of more than thirteen years. It is a treasure-trove of traditional stories, picked up near the stoves and kitchen-hearths of small German towns and villages, from peasant women who took no small pride in the vast number of stories they could tell without ever losing the thread of the narrative or confusing one tale with another. One of the most lustrous gems in their collection is the story of Hänsel and Gretel, which runs as follows:

A woodcutter with his wife and two children by a former marriage, a boy called Hänsel and a girl named Gretel, lives on the edge of a great forest. The woodcutter is exceedingly poor and often finds it difficult to earn enough money to buy food for his family. On one occasion, when starvation is staring them in the face, the stepmother suggests that, two mouths being easier to feed than four, they take the children into the thickest part of the forest, give each a piece of bread, leave them as if to go to work, and

thus be rid of them. The father, who is very fond
of his little boy and girl, objects at first, but is finally
prevailed upon to consent. Hänsel chances to over-
hear their plan, and as soon as his parents have fallen
asleep steals out of the house and gathers a large
number of pebbles. These he puts into his pocket,
and the next morning, when he and Gretel are led to
the forest, he drops one pebble after another upon
the path, unnoticed, to mark the road they travel.
When they reach the middle of the forest, the parents pretend that they are going to spend the day
cutting wood, and will return for the children at dusk,
when the work is done. Hänsel and Gretel wait
patiently but in vain. At last, with the bright moonlight shining upon the pebbles on the road, they succeed in finding their way home. The father rejoices
at their return, and the stepmother pretends that she
has been waiting for them. But soon thereafter,
when the larder is again empty, she once more in-
sists that they be rid of the children.

Again Hänsel overhears the plan to take them to
the forest on the morrow and determines to gather
more pebbles to mark the road; but the door is
locked and he cannot leave the house. He is full of
resource, however, and as the children accompany
their parents to the woods, Hänsel breaks the bread
that was given to him for his noonday meal and
strews the crumbs on the road. For the second time
the parents tell the children to await their return and

leave them. Hänsel and Gretel wait for night to
fall, expecting the same friendly moonlight to help
them find the crumbs on the road leading back
to their home; but, alas! the birds have eaten
all the crumbs and the children cannot find their
way.

They roam around the forest until from hunger
and exhaustion they fall asleep. Another day and
night are spent in the forest. On the third morning
they notice a white bird carolling on the bough of a
tall tree. When the song is finished the bird flies
off; they follow it and come to a cottage built of
bread and cakes, with window-panes of clear sugar.
The hungry children do not wait for a special invitation, but Hänsel immediately samples the roof of the
tempting house and Gretel one of its windows. A
voice from within demands to know who is nibbling
at the house; the door opens, and an old woman
welcomes the children and invites them to enter.
They are well fed and tucked into cosy beds, but the
next day the woman, who is really a witch and eats
all children who fall into her power, shows her true
colours. She puts Hänsel into a cage and proceeds to
fatten him with all kinds of delicacies. Gretel fares
rather worse; she is fed on scraps and compelled to
tend the oven in which she and Hänsel are to be
baked, savoury morsels for the cruel witch. Gretel is
a clever little girl, however, and when the witch in-
quires whether the oven is hot enough, she pretends

not to know and asks the witch to show her how to
find out. The witch undertakes to instruct Gretel,
but as she puts her head into the oven Gretel pushes
her in, shuts the door, and the witch is burned to
death in her own oven. Then Gretel opens Hänsel's
cage, and together they explore the cottage, which
they find full of jewels and precious stones. Hänsel
fills his pockets with them; Gretel gathers all she
can into her apron, and they depart.

After walking a few hours they reach a sheet of
water too wide and deep for them to ford, so Hänsel
calls to a duck that is swimming near and begs to be
carried across. The duck takes them to the other
side, where they find a road that soon becomes familiar and leads them, without further adventure, to
their home. Their father is overjoyed at their return,
and their stepmother is dead. Hänsel empties his
pockets and Gretel her apron of the treasures taken
from the witch's cottage, and they live happily ever
after.

Thus their story as told by Grimm. Its great age is
testified to by the *motif* of cannibalism which appears
in it and by the fact that variants of the same tale are
found in the folktales of nations as widely separated
as are the Persians and Lapps, the Portuguese and
Magyars, pointing to its origin at a time when, long
before the migrations of the peoples, the common
ancestors of all listened to it in their Eastern home.

Special interest attaches to the Magyar version,

combining the story of Hänsel and Gretel with that
of Cinderella* somewhat as follows:

The three daughters of a very poor king have become too great a burden for their stepmother and are
to be taken to the thickest part of a vast forest, there
to be left to their fate. The youngest daughter overhears the plot and consults her grandmother as to the
best means of escape. The grandmother gives her a
spool of thread to unwind along their path, thus en-
abling her to lead her sisters back home. On the
second occasion she receives a bag of ashes to strew
over the road, and again they are able to return.
The third time the girl decides that she needs no
advice and takes a bag of peas; but when she tries
to find the way the birds have eaten all the peas.
Three days and three nights the sisters roam the
woods before they come to a large castle. They enter
and are terrified to see a giantess, who greets them
with the words: "What a splendid roast you will
make!" They gain a reprieve from such a dreadful
fate by a promise to make beautiful garments for the
giantess; but as soon as the giant arrives he smells
human flesh and orders his wife to produce it unless
she would herself be devoured. The girls promise
the giant that they will bake and cook for him and
are spared for the time being. But their real hope
lies in the fact that the giant and giantess are unwill-

*It is interesting to note that of the story of Cinderella 318
variants have been found.

ing to divide, each desiring the whole of this choice repast for himself. As the maidens are preparing the feast which they have promised, the youngest asks the giant to see if the fire is hot enough, and as he puts his head into the oven he is pushed in and burned to death.

The giantess is furious at first, but before wreaking vengeance on the sisters, and incidentally obtaining the coveted feast, she permits the girls to beautify her. The youngest sister, while dressing the giantess' hair, drives an iron comb into her head and kills her. After the maidens have taken possession of the castle the two oldest sisters begin to treat the youngest harshly, making her render menial service while they enjoy themselves. One day, when her sisters have gone to a dance in the neighbourhood, the youngest sister, in cleaning a chimney, finds a golden key which opens a closet full of finery. She attires herself in costly garments and hurries to the dance, where she is the cynosure of all eyes. She leaves before the dance is over, and when her sisters return home she receives them in her servant's clothes. The sisters brag about their success at the dance until some impudent female arrived and put them in the background; and they beat the youngest sister when she suggests that she herself might have been the beautiful stranger who attracted every one's attention.

The same thing occurs the following week. On the third Sunday the girl, hurrying to leave the dance in time to get home before her sisters, loses one of her slippers, which is picked up by the prince, who has fallen in love with her. A grave illness seizes the prince. The court physician pronounces him lovesick, and says that he must die unless he finds the object of his affection. The King promises that he may marry his love whoever she be, and the prince declares it is the owner of the slipper. So all the maidens in the kingdom are bidden to appear at court to try it on, but the slipper is too small for every one except the youngest sister, who, moreover, proves her identity by producing its mate. She consents to marry the prince on condition that her father's conquered kingdom be restored to him, and this is done. She is proclaimed Queen, and her sisters are sent back to their father's court, where, the story says, they are still living if they have not since died.

In adapting the story of Hänsel and Gretel to the requirements of an opera book, Mrs. Wette, the composer's sister, has wisely and successfully heeded our modern ideas of what a story written for children and about children should be. The element of cruelty has been eliminated by making the stepmother the children's real mother who sends them to the forest, not in order to let them perish, but for the purpose of gathering berries to take the place of the supper that has been spoiled. The idea of cannibalism, surviving in the Grimm tale, is softened by making the witch turn into gingerbread all children who fall into her clutches—a device entirely consistent with the character of the story, inasmuch as the metamorphosis of human beings into animals or inanimate things is frequently met with in folklore. It is, moreover, very felicitous in that it offers the opportunity for bringing back to life the witch's previous victims.

The action of the play also derives great additional charm from the dream pantomime, with the vision of the angels protecting the children who are asleep in the woods. The finale, with the joyous reunion of Hänsel and Gretel and the parents who have set out in search of them, provides the happy ending which is an essential of every true *Märchen*.

THE close of the nineteenth century witnessed the inception of a world-wide movement centering about the child; and his development in every direction—mental, physical and moral—began to be newly studied. To this movement not only Science but Art as well contributed its share. The literature for the young was written from a new viewpoint as the responsibilities of Art toward the child began to be realized. No author's best seemed too good, no poet's finest too fine, no illustrator's choicest too choice for the formation of the growing mind. Kipling's Jungle Book and Stevenson's Child's Garden of Verses, the drawings of Boutet de Monvel and Maxfield Parrish are significant of the new spirit. And in music, too, there came a change, best signalised by Engelbert Humperdinck's fairy opera of Hänsel and Gretel.

This work brought the composer, hitherto comparatively unknown, into great prominence, and its success was immediate and universal. Just twenty years before the public, it has already become a classic, making its appeal to the largest possible audience, one which includes not only children but all the adults who are fortunate enough to have carried something of the spirit of youth beyond the border of maturity.

Just as the material for the libretto was taken from one of the tales which had its origin in the childhood of the race, so the composer, too, drew his inspiration from the folk-songs of Germany, a fruitful source which had already been successfully tapped by

Carl Maria von Weber. The combination was so
felicitous and so obvious that it is hard to realize now
that this was practically a new venture in the operatic
world. Wagner had pointed the way to the storehouse
of mythology; Humperdinck discovered the by-path
to fairyland.

The dominant characteristic of Humperdinck's
music is its sincerity. That, too, is the basis of the
eternal appeal of the folk-song. One can no more
think of Hänsel and Gretel as written by an English-
man, a Frenchman or an Italian, than he could imagine
the little nursery song "Susie, dearest Susie" (Suse,
liebe Suse) flowering out of English, French or
Italian soil. As in the case of Grieg and his Norse
melodies, so indigenous is Humperdinck's music that
it is difficult to eradicate the false but general notion
that most of it is directly derived from genuine folk-
tunes. In a sense this is true of Humperdinck as it
was of Grieg, for many of their finest melodies are
patterned on the lines of the folk-song from which
they gathered their inspiration. And in the case
of Humperdinck the occasional use of an actual
folk-song serves naturally to mislead the listener
into the belief that none of the music is wholly
original.

In Hänsel and Gretel there are four genuine *Volks-
Melodien:* the first song of the children (Suse, liebe
Suse), the Broom Venders' call, the little song sung
by Gretel at the opening of the second act, and the

horn-call with which the prelude to the third act opens. The rest of the music is wholly original.

Nevertheless, the composer has ingeniously drawn some of his new melodic material from the first two of these. A musical illustration will best explain this:

The root of the tune "Susie, dearest Susie" is

In the children's dance we have first this phrase:

and then this variant:

The Broom-maker's song also starts with this theme (in the minor key) :

while the witch herself, doubtless to signify her child-like joy in riding the broomstick, is accompanied by almost the identical phrase:

An old Rhenish call, used by itinerant venders in plying their trade (and first sung in the opera by the

Broom-maker in his recital of how he disposed of
his wares) :

Kauf Be · sen

is the basis of the movement of the Witch's Ride.

Nor does it require much stretch of the imagination to see in the little song which Gretel sings, "A
silent mankin stands in the woods at rest" (Ein
Männlein steht im Walde, ganz still und stumm) :

the suggestion for the Garland Motive:

And what could be more appropriate and suggestive,
since the "Silent Mankin," whom the folk-song de-
scribes is the *Hagebutte* or fruit of a little wood-
land flower like our wild rose, of which Gretel is
weaving her garland.

There is a natural curiosity and interest in studying
the workings of genius and in isolating the germ which
the creative power selects and develops anew; and it
is in this spirit that the analysis of the music of Hänsel and Gretel should be undertaken. Humperdinck's

method of theme treatment is the same as that pursued by the great symphonic writers. The *leit-motiv* is employed in Hänsel and Gretel quite as consistently as in the early works of Wagner, though with none of the elaboration or complexity of detail of the later Wagner dramas or of Humperdinck's own "Königskinder."

The musical illustrations given above show in some slight way how the composer worked. An additional example may not come amiss. There is a melodic root, so to say, of three notes, which is constantly employed in connection with the Witch's music.

They appear in the Witch's Ride:

and again in the Enticement theme in its varying forms:

And

Finally they appear in the Gingerbread Waltz, in which is celebrated the undoing of the Witch:

Humperdinck brought to the treatment of the little nursery tale the full Wagnerian equipment of orchestra and technique. There is the same use of the continuous melody and declamatory style and the same general harmonic and structural scheme. The same method which Wagner devised as an accompaniment to the passions of Isolde and the woes of Brünnhilde is here employed to give musical utterance to the playfulness and the trifling griefs and fears of Hänsel and Gretel. The heroic ride of the Valkyries is painted in colours no more brilliant than the broomstick ride of the Witch. The incongruity between means and end is glaring. Yet, wonder of wonders! the criticism once made, it is forgotten in the all-pervading charm and sincerity of the work.

The music is constructed with a wealth of detail that wholly escapes the casual listener, but affords keen pleasure to the musician. The contrapuntal ingenuity, the technical mastery of means and the great artistic restraint are notable throughout. But above all and, in view of the vast expenditure of scholarship and skill, most remarkable of all, there are abundant poetry and warmth of feeling and imagination, combined with directness and simplicity which imbue the music with ineradicable loveliness.

The appended extract arranged from the orchestral score will serve to illustrate the contrast between its apparent simplicity and actual complexity. It is from the Gingerbread Waltz; and it is safe to say

that no ordinary observer, carried along by the fine,
free, melodious swing, ever by any possible chance

Enticement (18), imitating in canon form the same theme in the bass.

suspects that it is constructed of five distinct component parts, all running along simultaneously but without any clash. There is not the slightest overloading of detail; yet the skill with which the contrapuntal web is woven is a marvel as well as a delight to the musician. For its equal in technical mastery and apparent effortlessness, we must go back to the Finale of Mozart's "Jupiter" Symphony.

NOTE

The first appearance of each theme is marked by the music in the body of the text and the number of the theme on the left of the music. Every recurrence is noted in the text at the point in the narrative where it appears.

PART III

GUIDE TO THE OPERA

THE PRELUDE

The Prelude to Hänsel and Gretel is something more than the usual introduction to the music of the score. It is in itself a complete musical entity, an epitome of one phase of the story. It ignores completely all musical reference to the mother's anger, the children's fear of the forest, and the mock terrors inspired by the witch. There is in it no hint of sadness, real or imagined. Instead of all this, there is a reproduction of all the high lights of the opera, its humours and gay exuberances, its guardian angels and sheltering forests.

It commences, unaffectedly and without preliminaries, with the EVENSONG (2), to whose reverent harmonies the two children, wandering in the forest, compose themselves for peaceful slumber. Four horns intone the theme in four-part harmony; it is like one of the old Church Chorales, full of aspiration and latent power, welling up through the orchestra, sonorous, yet never loud, then diminishing as it is carried still on and upward to the highest reaches of the instruments. There it is finally broken off by a trumpet call indicative of the COUNTERCHARM (24) with which the dangers and difficulties that beset the children's path are at last met and mastered.

This theme, which is an inversion of the Hocus-

Pocus formula or SPELL (23) by which the witch enchants her victims, illustrates aptly, by a musical device, the notion of the subversion of the magic charm. After an elaborate development of the COUNTERCHARM (24), a new melody is heard. It is the song of THE MORNING (19) with which the Dewman wakens the sleeping children, and it carries with it such a sense of sunshine and cool breezes as to suggest the thought that light and sun and nature's freshness are the best of countercharms to darkness and witchery.

Immediately following the MORNING SONG (19) comes the theme of DELIVERANCE (26). It is used near the close of the opera when the children have forever rid themselves and the enchanted gingerbread boys and girls (who, less fortunate than they, had not escaped the witch's craft) from the malign influence of her evil spirit.

And now, characteristically, the composer combines all of this melodic material with marvellous skill and a no less marvellous appearance of simplicity, naturalness and inevitability. The EVEN-SONG (2) is again heard, as at first, but is quickly developed and disguised by its use in augmented and diminished time. In one place, indeed, it is given simultaneously in three distinct forms. Meanwhile the COUNTERCHARM (24), MORNING SONG (19), and DELIVERANCE (26) are playfully bandied back and forth. There are sudden contrasts, alternate light and shade, artfully prepared harmonic changes, and an ever-increasing complexity of texture, until, after a magnificent climax, the music again becomes quietly reserved, simple and direct, and the Prelude closes with a return to the EVENSONG (2), which, dying away to a pianissimo, finally vanishes into thin air.

ACT I

ONCE upon a time, not so very long ago, a Broom-maker lived with his wife and two children in a tiny cottage that stood at the edge of a great forest. They were very, very poor; so poor, indeed, that they did not always have enough to eat, although the Broommaker worked all day and every day, fashioning his wares and travelling through the neighbouring villages to sell them, while his wife washed and swept and mended and cooked—when there was anything in the house to be cooked.

Even the children were taught to do their small share of work towards the family's maintenance, and on the day on which the opera story opens Hänsel and Gretel are busy at their tasks. The room in which they sit is shabbily and sparsely furnished. The only ornaments are the brooms of various sizes ranged along the walls. On one side is a window through which the great trees of the adjacent forest are easily visible. On another is a fireplace with a crude chimney above it. It is near this, on a low stool, that Gretel sits, busily knitting a stocking, while opposite to her, near the door, Hänsel bends over his broom-making.

The day has been a lonely one for the children. Their father has gone on his rounds; their mother is away on an errand, and—worst of all—there has been nothing to eat. But Hänsel and Gretel are brave

little folk and accustomed to the trials of poverty;
so, instead of weeping and wailing, as other children
might have done, they try to forget their hunger by
singing an old, old nursery song:

"Susie, dearest Susie, what stirs in the hay?
　The geese are going barefoot,
　And no shoes have they.
　The cobbler has leather,
　But no last to use,
　And that's the reason why geese must go
　　without shoes."

(Suse, liebe Suse, was raschelt im Stroh?
　Die Gänse geh'n barfuss und haben kein' Schuh.
Der Schuster hat's Leder, kein'n Leisten dazu,
　Drum kann er den Gänslein auch machen kein'
　　Schuh.)

The theme of this song is used all through the
opera to typify the children: CHILDHOOD (1)

(1)

It varies in expression as the moods of the children
change. With them it is gay and cheerful or sad and
troubled. Yet, however it comes, it carries with it
the sense of irresponsibility and freeheartedness which
is the mark of childhood.

As the children finish the song, Hänsel's patience
comes to an end. He throws his unfinished broom

into a corner and jumps up. "Oh, if mother would only come home," he cries. "Nothing to eat for weeks but dry bread."

Gretel tries to calm and comfort him, reminding him of the words their father has so often spoken:

> "When your need is at its height,
> God will set all things aright."

> (Wenn die Not auf's höchste steigt,
> Gott der Herr die Hand euch reicht.)

These words are sung to the tune of the EVENSONG (2) with which the Prelude opened:

(2)

But its tenderness and faith do not serve to convince Hänsel, and the motive of CHILDHOOD (1) reappears as he declares that faith will not satisfy hunger. The poor boy is very near to tears, and it requires all the persistence and good cheer that Gretel can muster to induce him to forget his troubles and join in a jolly song to banish the spirit of the Grumbler. A big broom is brought into playful service to aid in the work, and the experiment soon proves entirely successful.

The children renew their gaiety as Gretel, to a charming variant of the CHILDHOOD (1) motive, confides to Hänsel the wonderful secret that a kindly neighbour has sent them a jug of milk, which their mother, when she comes home, may well be counted upon to use for a tempting rice-pudding. Hänsel shouts with boyish glee at the mere thought of anything so rare and delightful; and his laughter is indicated by a rippling figure which can hardly be called a motive and yet is worthy of mention because it is used in several other places in the course of the opera to depict the spontaneous laughter of the children and also of the father, whose spirit is so much like theirs.

Gretel soon finds, indeed, that in her effort to drive away Hänsel's tears she has driven Hänsel himself to the extreme of hilarity. The orchestra sounds the CHILDHOOD (1) theme sharply and warningly (in the minor) ; and we suspect that trouble is brewing when Hänsel puts his finger into the milk-bowl and Gretel slaps the offending hand, ordering the boy to go back to his broommaking so that they need not fear to be punished for idleness when their mother comes home.

But now all of Gretel's worries cannot affect Hänsel's gay humour. He declares that work is out of the question. "Let us dance!" he cries; "let us be merry!" and Gretel succumbs to the temptation. Once more the CHILDHOOD (1) theme resumes its cheery tone and runs merrily into the music of the dance, as Gretel begins:

"Brother, come and dance with me,
Both my hands I give to thee;
This way one, that way two,
Round about, that's all's to do."

(Brüderchen, komm tanz mit mir,
Beide Händchen reich ich dir.
Einmal hin, einmal her,
Rund herum, es ist nicht schwer.)

The words are those of a favourite folk-song, but
the melody is Humperdinck's own, and is one of the
brightest as well as the most popular in the whole
opera.

(3)

To this Hänsel replies:

"You would have me dance and bow,
Sister, when I don't know how.
Show a fellow what to do,
So that I can dance like you."

(Tanzen soll ich armer Wicht,
Schwesterlein, und kann es nicht.
Darum zeig' mir, wie es Brauch,
Dass ich tanzen lerne auch.)

Hänsel's answer is set to a second melody. In
fact, the DANCE (3) can hardly be spoken of as having a melody. Rather, it has a succession of lovely

melodies, each gayer and more irresistible than the
last, one following fast upon the heels of the other,
and, while not connected organically, all so cleverly
combined that they form a perfect melodic whole.
The entire music of this scene is a web of these melodies as the boy and girl, hand in hand, circle more
and more wildly about, until in their exuberance they
stumble over each other and fall to the floor.

Just at this moment their mother enters, empty
basket in hand. The children jump up frightened,
and the CHILDHOOD (1) theme, in the minor, as
might well be expected, accompanies their futile attempts to explain to their mother's satisfaction the
reason why their work remains undone. The mother
is very, very angry; rushes for a rod to whip the
children, and in her haste knocks over the jug of milk,
breaking it to pieces and spilling the precious contents. The tears come to her eyes, and when she
hears Hänsel giggling at her distress she loses the
last vestige of patience. Giving the children the
basket, she pushes them out of the door, telling them
to go to the woods and not to return until the basket
is full of berries.

It is a rash thing to do when the day is nearly spent
and the shadows of the mighty forest trees are already
beginning to lengthen. And yet the mother does not
lack our sympathy as she sits down exhausted beside
the table and recounts her miseries. The motive of
CHILDHOOD (1) in the accompaniment shows but too

clearly that her sorrow is not for the broken jug, not
for herself or her own hunger, but for the little son
and daughter who share her want.   So she falls
asleep.

For a moment there is silence, only a horn droning
out a lonely note.   Then from the distance comes the
sound of a man's voice singing:

> "Ah, the poor man's life is dreary,
> Every day seems long and weary.
> Not one coin his purse conceals,
> Empty quite his stomach feels.
> Rallalala, rallalala,
> Hungry folk enjoy their meals."

> (Ach, wir armen, armen Leute!
> Alle Tage so wie Heute:
> In dem Beutel ein grosses Loch
> Und im Magen ein gröss'res noch—
> Rallalala, Rallalala,
> Hunger ist der beste Koch.)

(4)

The song begins with a phrase of the same melodic
contour as the CHILDHOOD (1) motive.   And the
resemblance is easily accounted for, since the Broommaker who sings it is still so much of a child in spirit
that even the refrain of his song, "Hungry folk enjoy
their meals," carries with it more of frolic than of

tragedy. In a moment the Broommaker's jovial face
appears at the window and, still singing, he comes into
the room, bending under the weight of the basket he
carries on his back. His song is elaborately worked
out through all the stanzas, turned, twisted, now gay,
now complaining, but always coming back to its
original conclusion.

"Rallalala, rallalala, Hungry folk enjoy their meals,"
   (Rallalala, rallalala, Hunger ist der beste Koch,)

(5)

Ral-la-la-la, ral-la-la-la, Hunger ist der beste Koch.

until, at last, with the old fellow's admission that
"Kimmel is my favourite drink" (Kümmel ist mein
Leiblikör), the suspicion that his excessive gaiety is
due to something besides his own good nature is
confirmed.

He goes—a bit unsteadily—to where his wife is
sitting and wakens her with a resounding kiss. Her
husband's merry humour, the cause of which she
quickly discerns, seems to the poor woman only an
added misery, and when he asks for supper she fairly
loses her temper and says:

> "Most simple is the bill of fare,
> The evening meal is—heaven knows where.
> Platter bare,
> Cellar bare,
> The purse is empty and nothing there."

(Höchst einfach ist das Speisregister,
Der Abendschmaus—zum Henker ist er.
Teller leer,
Keller leer,
Und im Beutel ist gar nichts mehr.)

But the Broommaker has the best of remedies for
such an ill, and, opening his basket, he discloses to the
eyes of his astonished wife his accumulated store of
goodies.

"Husband," she cries, "what do I see?" (Mann,
was seh ich?) and, by way of further response, the
broommaker turns the basket upside down and lets
the contents roll out on the floor. Many a long day
it is since the poor kitchen has seen such a feast and
the Mother's delight knows no bounds. With a glee
quite equal to that of the children she takes her husband's hands and dances with him around the room.
But, after a moment, the housewife's instincts revive,
and while she carefully puts the stores into the cup-
board, lights the fire on the hearth and begins beat-
ing eggs in a bowl, her husband sits beside her telling
how the wonder came about. He tells how he came
to the town beyond the woods and found the people
making preparations for a great feast. There were
to be weddings, a kirmess and celebrations of all
kinds (and here the music lends colour to his tale by
suggesting the movement of the children's dance).

Of course, continues the Broommaker, who would

hold a feast must first clean and sweep and scrub, so there, ready to hand, was a special market for his wares, and all he needed to do was to go from house to house, calling

"Buy besoms! Good sweepers!"

(Kauft Besen! Gute Feger!)

(6)

The call he uses is said to be traditional with Rhenish broommakers, and the composer soon gives it a humorous turn in connection with the Witch's Ride.

The Broommaker finishes his story, and pots and pans are made ready for the best of suppers, before he remembers to ask for Hänsel and Gretel. The theme of CHILDHOOD (1) sounds abruptly. The Mother declares that she does not know where the children are; the only thing she does know is that the new jug is broken. She relates how she came home to find the children idle and in mischief, and the DANCE (3) refrain in the orchestra hints at what the mischief was. Even at a distance, she says, she could hear Hänsel and Gretel laughing and shouting, and hopping and dancing like young colts, until from very anger——

"The jug broke," interrupts the Broommaker, who, with quick intuition, sees the humour in the situa-

tion and breaks into the same rippling laughter figure
which Hänsel has made familiar.

His good nature calms the Mother's anger and
yet, when he repeats his question about the children's
whereabouts, she answers curtly,

"For aught I care, at the Ilsenstein."

(Meinethalben am Ilsenstein.)

The Broommaker becomes serious at once and is
visibly alarmed. He goes to the wall and takes down
a broom. "BUY BESOMS" (6) call the woodwinds,
while the strings reminisce of the children's DANCE
(3). The Mother orders him to put the broom back
where it belongs.

In the orchestra comes a solemn chord progression
eloquently suggestive of the MYSTERIES OF THE
FOREST (7):

The Broommaker drops the broom he holds and
wrings his hands, crying aloud that the children may
be lost in the woods where the Evil One dwells.

"The Evil One!" says the Mother, surprised, and
the BROOM CALL (6) becomes more persistent, more
definite, renewing more forcibly its prophetic suggestion of the Witch's Ride, as the Father whispers,
meaningly, "The Nibble-Witch" (Die Knusperhexe).

The Mother shrinks back in terror, whispering after him the words, "The Nibble-Witch," and asking, frightened, what the broom may mean in all this. "The Broom," repeats the Father in the significant words of the old saw, "THE BROOM, THE BROOM, PRAY WHAT IS IT FOR?" (8).

(8)

The music answers first with the full wild theme of the WITCH'S RIDE (9):

(9)

and the Broommaker bursts out, in fearsome eloquence, with the BALLAD OF THE WITCH (10):

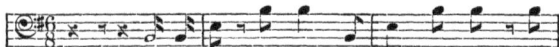

Ei-ne Hex' steinalt haust tief im wald, Vom

(10)

Teu - fel sel - ber hat sie Ge-walt!

"The besom, the besom,
    Pray what is it for? Pray, what is it for?
    On it there ride, on it there ride
    The witches.
    A witch age-old,
    Dwells deep i' the wold,

From Satan's self her power doth hold.
Midnight she bides,
Hush on all sides,
Then forth to the witch's dance she rides.
Through the chimney-pot
She flies from the cot,
On the broom, O gloom, at a gallop and trot.
Over hill and dale,
Over mount and vale,
Through a misty veil,
Through the air in a gale,
That's how they ride, that's how they ride,
Ohé! Ohé! The witches!"

(Der Besen! Der Besen!
Was macht man damit? Was macht man
    damit?
Es reiten drauf, es reiten drauf
Die Hexen!
Eine Hex' steinalt,
Haust tief im Wald,
Vom Teufel selber hat sie Gewalt!
Um Mitternacht,
Wann niemand wacht,
Dann reitet sie aus zur Hexenjagd,
Zum Schornstein hinaus
Entschlüpft sie dem Haus,
Auf dem Besen, O Graus; in Saus und
    Braus!

Über Berg und Kluft,
Über Thal und Gruft,
Durch Nebelduft,
Im Sturm durch die Luft:
Ja so reiten, ja so reiten,
Juchheissa, die Hexen!)

In the second stanza the Broommaker tells of the
poor children who are lured into the Witch's cottage
and transformed into gingerbread; and the CHILD-
HOOD (1) motive changes to a new figure, which
grows and grows with the Mother's growing fear
for her children until it fills the orchestra and fairly
overflows as the terrified woman runs out of the
house. The Broommaker hesitates just long enough
to pick up his flask from the table. Then the memory
of the children's danger, still insisted upon in the
orchestra, overcomes him too, and he rushes out
after his wife as the curtain falls.

THE WITCH'S RIDE

There is no break in the music between the First and Second Acts, the scenic pause being filled by a symphonic interlude, called the WITCH'S RIDE (9) and entirely descriptive. The melodic material of which it is constructed consists of the BROOM VENDER'S CALL (6), the BESOM (8), and the theme of the WITCH'S RIDE (9). The spirit of the music is that of mock terror, and the orchestral colouring is skilfully designed to convey this feeling. There is vim and verve aplenty, and the unrestrained glee of the witch astride her broomstick is vividly presented. With no hint of musical resemblance, the piece is, nevertheless, a Ride of the Valkyries in playful terms of magic. After a final fling, the ride stops and the music drops suddenly into the theme of the FOREST (13), sounded tranquilly, in soft trumpet tones. With a parting reminiscence of the WITCH'S RIDE (9) the movement draws to a close and prepares for the rise of the curtain with echoing calls from the woodwinds and horns.

ACT II

THE scene shows a slight clearing in the forest. In the background is the Ilsenstein, majestically rising out of its dense covering of fir-trees. Gretel is sitting on a moss-covered trunk in the shadow of one of the great firs, weaving a garland of wild flowers. On the ground beside her is a posy of freshly gathered blossoms. Hänsel is busy hunting berries in the bushes at the other side of the clearing. It is twilight, and a sense of peace and tranquillity is over everything. Gretel is singing a beautiful folk-song whose eternal charm Humperdinck has heightened by his delightful and poetic accompaniment:

"A silent mankin stands in the woods at rest,
  Pure crimson is the mantle in which he's dressed.
  Tell me, who the man may be,
  Standing there so silently,
  Wrapped in crimson mantle, from head to knee?"

(Ein Männlein steht im Walde
Ganz still und stumm;
Es hat von lauter Purpur
Ein Mäntlein um.
Sagt, wer mag das Männlein sein,
Das da steht im Wald allein,
Mit dem purpurroten Mäntelein?)

(11)

As Gretel ends her song, Hänsel puts one final berry
into his basket and, swinging it high in the air, comes
triumphantly to his sister. "My basket is full!" he
cries, and, by way of response, Gretel shows him her
lovely garland which is just completed. The orchestra sounds the GARLAND (12) theme

(12)

and bears it along into the scene as Gretel tries to put
the garland on Hänsel's head, and he scorns the offer-
ing, insisting that such things are not for boys but for
maidens. Gretel allows herself to be crowned, and
then, when Hänsel declares that she looks like the
Queen of the Forest, she laughingly commands him
to present the posy to the Queen, a gift which he,
kneeling with playful homage, gaily supplements by
the precious basket of berries.

It is true that he warns Gretel not to eat any; but
just at that moment a cuckoo call is heard and the
children, imitating him and accusing him of all the
vices the poor bird is supposed to possess, soon fall into
their gay way of transforming everything into a game
and, pretending to be cuckoos themselves, they devour
the berries as the cuckoo devours the eggs he steals
from other birds' nests.

Still the GARLAND (12) melody continues. The
game goes on more and more hilariously. Above the

voices of the children the call of the cuckoo is heard
from time to time, gradually disappearing; the twilight colours are fading from the sky, and as Hänsel,
in a final burst of merriment, puts the basket to his
mouth and empties it of its few remaining berries,
the darkness seems suddenly to fall.

Gretel snatches the basket from Hänsel's hand.
"What have you done?" she cries. "Oh, how we
shall be punished for this!" Hänsel is unperturbed.
"You did it, too," he tells her; but when she urges
him to come quickly and gather more berries his mood
changes as he realizes that it is too late.

"Hark!" he whispers, "how it rustles in the trees.
Do you know what the forest says? Children," it
says, "are you not afraid?" (Horch, wie rauscht es in
den Bäumen! Weisst du, was der Wald jetzt spricht?
Kindlein," sagt er, "fürchtet ihr euch nicht?")

The motive of the FOREST (13) is intoned, a
melody broad, restful, all-embracing, symbolical of
the sheltering guardianship of the great, green
dwellers of the woods.

(13)

Again the theme sounds in the English horns and
then, as Hänsel admits that he has lost the way, the
first half of the motive is changed, and the music,
losing its restfulness and charm, becomes significant

of the TERRORS OF THE FOREST (14) and the evil
spirits that beset it at night.

(14)

The shadows of the white birches, which Gretel
mistakes for witches astride their brooms; the flicker-
ing of fireflies; the gradually disappearing echo, like
the parting cuckoo call, are all suggested in the musical
colouration. The children become more and more
fearful, clinging to each other as the shadows deepen.
At last Gretel bursts into tears. Hänsel tries to
comfort her. "Gretel," he says, "cling close to me.
I will protect you." The MYSTERY OF THE FOREST
(7) is repeated, that strange and suggestive harmonic
progression which accompanied the father's words
when he expressed his dread lest the children be lost
in the forest.

A thick mist rises and entirely shuts out the background. Gretel thinks she sees the form of the cloud
women approaching, nodding and beckoning. She
screams and rushes, panic-stricken, to hide herself
under a fir-tree. Just then there is a rift in the cloud,
and a little gray man with a tiny sack on his back
appears.

He comes towards the children in such a friendly
way that he sets all their fears at rest. At once the
character of the music changes. Even the TERRORS

OF THE FOREST (14), played by the soft-sounding
harp, takes on a soothing tone. As the little man
advances he throws tiny grains of sand into the children's eyes and sings "I am the Little Sandman,"

(15)

ending his song with the PROMISE (16):

"And when you've fallen sound asleep,
  The stars will all arise,
And little angels will come down
  From heaven's high emprise.
The bearers of sweet dreams are they
So, children, dream away."

(Und seid ihr fein geschlafen ein,
  Dann wachen auf die Sterne,
Und nieder steigen Engelein
Aus hoher Himmelsferne,
  Und bringen holde Träume,
  Drum träume, Kindchen, träume.)

(16)

The song culminates musically, too, in this broad
cantilena which accompanies the PROMISE (16) of
safety and beautiful dreams, and so the little Sandman

disappears, and everything is shrouded in darkness. Hänsel, half-asleep, says, "The Sandman has been here," and Gretel rouses herself just enough to answer, "Let us say our evening prayer." Side by side the children kneel and fold their hands. The words they sing are those of a children's prayer that has come down from olden times. The original music has been lost, but it is doubtful if it was more beautiful and fitting than the melody which the composer has created for it. This EVENSONG (2) melody has already been heard in the opening of the Prelude to the opera, in the form of a Chorale assigned to the horns, but it gains an added significance in this lovely setting.

The children sink back on the moss and fall asleep. The orchestra continues the music of the EVENSONG (2), taking it up, through the instruments, as though carrying the prayer to heaven, and as the music reaches the highest point the answer seems to come in a ray of silver light breaking through the cloud which obscured the background. Again the forest is illumined and the theme of the FOREST (13) reappears as the clouds roll together to form a disappearing stairway in the middle of the stage. Down these stairs come the angels whom the Sandman promised, fourteen of them, two by two, the smallest first, taking their places around the sleeping children.

The music that accompanies this beautiful dream-pantomime represents the high water mark of the opera. It opens with the PROMISE (16), and this and the theme of the EVENSONG (2) in diminished time form the melodic material of which the episode is constructed. The movement, which fairly mounts upwards in the fullness of its beauty, reaches its climax with the trumpets and trombones sounding the EVENSONG (2) in strong, simple, stirring chords. The entire scene, apparently so simple and naive, yet withal so profoundly erudite in its treatment, is eminently typical of Humperdinck.

When the picturesque circle formed by the fourteen winged figures is complete, the music gradually resolves itself back to the EVENSONG (2) in its simplest form, and the curtain falls.

ACT III

THE Introduction to the Third Act shows no trace
of the lovely music of the dream, no memory of angels
or of sheltering forests. It opens boldly with the
NIBBLING (17) theme, a crisp horn call, which, without its final and determining note, is soon discovered
to be nothing more than the almost universal nursery
theme known to English-speaking folk as "Ring-a-
ring-a-rosy."

(17)

The composer's choice of so harmless a melody to
typify the witch who inspired the Broommaker with
such fear is assurance enough that she will not prove
very dangerous to Hänsel and Gretel. Over and
over the NIBBLE (17) is repeated, first simply and
alone, then combined with the motive of ENTICE-
MENT (18) in one of the many forms in which it is
to show itself before the story ends.

(18)

The motive of MORNING (19) is heard.

(19)

Slowly the curtain rises. The scene is the same as
that upon which the second act closed. The background is still shrouded in mist, which is gradually
lifting. The only change is that the angels have disappeared with the vanishing night. In their place
the Dewman, who accompanies the dawn, comes with
his pretty bluebell, from whose cup he sprinkles dew-
drops on the little sleepers. As Hänsel and Gretel
bestir themselves, the Dewman sings his song, which
begins exactly like the Sandman's, so close are sleep
and waking. Then he goes quietly away, and Hänsel
turns over and falls asleep again.

But Gretel opens her eyes and sits up. She looks
around her, full of wonder and surprise, not knowing
where she is, not even sure whether she is awake or
still asleep. The motive of the FOREST (13) in the
low, mellow register of the clarinet, followed by the
theme of the MORNING (19), indicate her gradual
realization of the time and the place. Then, seeing
Hänsel, she bends over him and sings in his ear,
imitating the lark, the cock and the other early birds
that are already wide awake.

As Gretel sings, Hänsel gradually wakens, rubs his
eyes, yawns, stretches himself and then, suddenly en-
tering into Gretel's spirit, jumps up and joins gaily
in her song. They both agree that they have never
slept so well as out here under the trees, wrapped in
the MYSTERY OF THE FOREST (7). Then Gretel
remembers her dream and Hänsel his, and they com-

pare their visions and are more and more delighted
as they find how entirely they coincide. At the beginning of the relation there is a slight suggestion of
the music of the dream pantomime, which grows into
a more definite and persistent reminder as the dream
becomes clearer to the children, until at last the
theme of the PROMISE (16) is restated. "Fourteen
angels there were," says Gretel, and the scene ends
with a return to that phrase of the EVENSONG (2)
which accompanied the words "Fourteen angels watch
do keep" (Vierzehn Engel um mich stehn).

As Hänsel finishes his story he turns just in time
to see the vanishing of the last thin veil of mist.
There is a sudden and effective harmonic change to
mark the children's surprise when, instead of the
forest of firs that covered the Ilsenstein when they
went to sleep, they see, by the light of the rising sun,
a very different scene. There is a tiny cottage close
to the Ilsenstein. To the left of this there is a large
bake-oven; beside that, a great cage, and both of
these are connected with the house by a fence of
gingerbread children. The music is eloquently illus-
trative of Hänsel's and Gretel's delight as they stand
speechless for a moment and then break into song in
praise of this glory of glories.

Their song takes the form of an alluring waltz
movement which has come to be known among the
Germans by the very expressive but quite untrans-
latable name of NASCHWALZER (20), which might

be—but half successfully—paraphrased as the Waltz
of Forbidden Sweets.

(20)

It is small wonder that the children mistake the
tiny cottage made of cakes and tarts for the home of
some princess of the woods. The roof is all covered
with cookies, the windows are of sugar, the gables
lined with raisins. But what most keenly arouses
their anticipation is the hedge of gingerbread. We
hear the motive of ANTICIPATION (21):

(21)

joined to the theme of the NASCHWALZER (20), and
the two broaden into a brilliant climax. Hänsel and
Gretel are convinced that if the owner of so delightful
a dwelling were at home and were to see two hungry
children watching at her gate she would gladly invite
them in to share her feast. But since everything is
still, Hänsel decides that nobody is there and suggests to Gretel that they go boldly in.

Gretel is horrified at the idea, but the repetition of
the NASCHWALZER (20) shows how she is tempted.
With a sudden inspiration, indicated to us by the

theme of the EVENSONG (2), Hänsel declares that the angels must have sent all of this for their special delectation, and Gretel allows herself to be convinced.

"Let us nibble a bit at the tiny house," says the boy.

"Yes, let us nibble like two little mice," answers his sister. The motive of the EVENSONG (2) gives way to the music of the NASCHWALZER (20) as the children, first looking carefully around to see that nobody is watching, come back to the little house, where, after some hesitation, Hänsel breaks a bit of cake from the right corner. As he does so there comes a voice from within the cottage, singing to the tune of the NIBBLE (17) motive as it appeared in the Prelude to this act:

"Nibble, nibble, little mouse,
Who's nibbling at my little house?"

(Knusper, knusper, Knäuschen,
Wer knuspert mir am Häuschen?)

Hänsel drops his cake in fright, and both children stand silent a moment. At last Gretel says, timidly, "The Wind, the Wind," and Hänsel echoes her words. Then Gretel picks up the bit of cake again and takes a bite. Through all the rest of the scene— in which the children take turns in munching the cake and in singing its praise—the music of the NASCH-WALZER (20) continues. But when Hänsel, waxing brave, breaks another big slice from the wall, we

hear again the voice, inquiring, "Nibble, nibble, little
mouse, Who's nibbling at my little house?"

The children are too engrossed in their pleasures
to do more than repeat "The Wind, the Wind."
They do not notice the opening of a window, nor see
the witch peering out at them. Gaily they continue
their pranks, eating, teasing, snatching bits from each
other, unmindful even when the door opens and the
Witch comes out and advances slyly towards them.
But just as their merriment reaches such a height that
they burst out laughing, they are made unmistakably
aware of her presence, for the Witch throws a rope
around Hänsel's neck and her laughter resounds—
not in the rippling figure we know, but in a shrill,
cackling cadence.

The children are fairly petrified with fright, nor
are their fears allayed by the Witch's fondling and
her seemingly gracious words. Her double-edged
praise of their plump faces, and her declaration that
she fairly loves children enough to eat them are
cleverly echoed in the music. To the melody of the
NASCHWALZER (20) she bids them welcome; with
a new form of the ENTICEMENT (18), she announces
herself as a person most kindly disposed toward children and herself as innocent as a child. The motive
of CHILDHOOD (1) appearing in the orchestra sounds
strangely out of keeping, wedged in between the variants of the ENTICEMENT (18), with which her
attempts at blandishment are liberally dotted.

But Hänsel and Gretel remain unconvinced and
turn away from her in disgust. If they are not easily
appeased, however, neither is the Witch easily dis-
couraged. The Naschwalzer (20), the motive of
Anticipation (21), and a new one, the Invitation (22)

(22)   [musical notation]   etc.

melody are made to spin a web of temptation for the
children, as the hag uses every means in her power to
lure them on. And, gradually, out of the musical
skein one thread is drawn, a significant variant of the
Enticement (18) theme, suggestive of the Witch's
special lure—the gingerbread. Yet even this fails of
its purpose. The more she urges and promises, the
more the children mistrust her. At last Hänsel frees
himself from the rope and he and Gretel start to run
away.

But immediately the witch throws off the mask of
friendliness and shows herself in her true form.
With her staff she makes the sign of the Spell (23),
and a sudden darkness falls as she repeats the fearful
formula of enchantment by which both children are
rooted to the spot where they stand:

"Hocus, pocus, witch's darts,
When you move, the flood-wave starts
Neither forward go nor back,

Banned you are with glances black,
Head be tilted stiffly back."

(Hocus, pocus, Hexenschuss,
Rühr dich, und dich beisst der Fluss!
Nicht mehr vorwärts, nicht zurück,
Bann dich mit dem bösen Blick;
Kopf steh starr dir im Genick.)

(23)

Ho - cus po - cus   He - xen - schuss.

Then sparks begin to fly from the end of her staff
and, pointing this at Hänsel, who is unable to take his
eyes from the glitter, she forces him, spellbound and
unresisting, into the stable, where she locks him in.

The light of day reappears, but still Gretel stands
absolutely motionless, while the Witch, whose
thoughts—as the gingerbread variant of the ENTICE-
MENT (18) shows—are all on the gingerbread into
which Hänsel is soon to be transformed, laughs con-
tentedly. After a moment she limps into the house,
telling Gretel to be a good girl and prepare to feed
Hänsel on the almonds and raisins he needs to make
him fat.

Hänsel uses the occasion of the Witch's absence to
warn his sister to pretend to do the Witch's bidding,
but in reality to beware of all she commands. There
is barely time for him to conclude his warning before

the Witch is back, carrying a basket of almonds and raisins, which she throws to Hänsel.

Then she turns to Gretel and disenchants her with a juniper branch, using the COUNTERCHARM (24), spoken of in the Prelude to the opera (which is seen to be the SPELL (23) in reverse form) to accomplish her purpose,

(24)

and following it with the ENTICEMENT (18), hoping by its lure to induce Gretel to fall to work, preparing for the meal to which the Witch so eagerly looks forward.

Finally Gretel goes into the house, and Hänsel pretends to be asleep, the better to watch the Witch. The hag goes joyously about her business. She opens the oven door to test the fire, and finding it not hot enough to suit her purpose adds a few bits of wood and rubs her hands in delighted expectation. All the while, to variants of the ENTICEMENT (18) motive, she rehearses her plan to make Gretel put her head into the oven to measure its heat, and she gloats over the opportunity this will afford to push the girl into the oven and transform her into gingerbread. Gretel seems such a rarely tempting and delightful morsel that the idea fairly overcomes the Witch, and, in a paroxysm of evil glee, she grabs up a broom and rides

wildly around the house, with Hänsel listening se-
cretly and Gretel watching, unseen, at the little window. The WITCH'S RIDE (9) of the Interlude is
repeated almost in full and the Witch shouts loudly
as she rides:

> "Hurr, hop, hop, hop,
> With a gallop and trot,
> My besom nag,
> Hurr, hop, don't lag."

> (Hurr, hop, hop, hop,
> Galopp, galopp,
> Mein Besengaul,
> Hurr, hopp, nit faul.)

Then, dismounting from her broom, the Witch
limps over to Hänsel and with the NIBBLE (17)
motive as a suggestive background, she tickles the boy
with a broom straw to waken him.

"Show me your tongue," says the Witch, and,
pleased at what she sees, "Show me your finger," she
adds. But Hänsel puts out a thin stick instead, and
the nearsighted Witch, finding this uninviting, en-
twines the NIBBLE (17) and ENTICEMENT (18) motives, as in the Prelude to this act, as she calls to Gretel
to bring out more raisins and more almonds.

Gretel brings the basket and stands behind the
Witch. As the latter proceeds to feed Hänsel, Gretel
disenchants the boy with the juniper branch accord-
ing to a formula which, while not so potent as that

of an experienced witch, is strong enough to succeed.
The Witch next turns her attention to the oven, and
Hänsel, understanding only too well what the prep-
arations mean, tries to give Gretel a warning sign.

Again the music repeats the threatening combination of the NIBBLE (17) and ENTICEMENT (18)
motives as the Witch grows more and more eager for
Gretel's transformation. At last she opens the oven
door! By this time Hänsel is quite beside himself
with fear for his sister, and carefully pushing open
the stable door he whispers words of warning, repeat-
ing them over and over, while suggestions of the
NASCHWALZER (20) and ENTICEMENT (18) appear in the minor as the Witch urges Gretel on, and
Gretel, awkwardly, but with a seeming innocence,
responds to all she says.

At the final direction, however, Gretel pretends that
she is too stupid to understand, and, losing patience
with the girl, the Witch puts her own head into the
oven to illustrate the way to test the fire. At once
both children (for Hänsel has crept slyly forward)
give her a hearty push so that she falls headlong in.
Then they close the door with a bang and, rejoicing
that it is the Witch and not Gretel who is the victim,
the children rush into each other's arms, singing:

> "Hurrah, at last the Witch is dead,
>   Stonydead.
> And now are vanished fear and dread.

"Hurrah, at last the Witch is still,
  Mouseystill.
And now of cakes we'll have our fill.

"Hurrah, at last 'tis o'er, the gloom,
  Witch's gloom,
And evil charms have met their doom.

  "So merry be and bright,
    Dance in the firelight,
    Hold in the Witch's house,
    Happiest joy carouse,
    Hurrah, hurrah!"

(Juchhei, Nun ist die Hexe tot,
    Mausetot!
Nun ist geschwunden Angst und Not!

Juchhei! Nun ist die Hexe still,
    Mäuschenstill,
Und Kuchen giebt's die Hüll und Füll.

Juchhei! Nun ist zu End der Graus,
    Hexengraus!
Und böser Zauberspuk ist aus!

    Drum lasst uns fröhlich sein,
    Tanzen im Feuerschein,
    Halten im Knusperhaus,
    Herrlichsten Freudenschmaus!
    Juchhei! Juchhei!)

Here at last, in this "Knusperwalzer" or GINGER-
BREAD WALTZ (25), the final variant of the ENTICE-
MENT (18) motive, spoken of as emphasising the
Witch's special gingerbread lure, comes fully into its
own.

(25)

The music bears a close resemblance both to that
variant and to the WITCH'S RIDE (9). All three, in
fact, are soon seen to be founded on the same first
three notes, which, looking over the score, we perceive
to be the common root of all the music pertaining to
the Witch and her machinations.

The song ends, but the children continue to dance
to the accompaniment of an orchestral interlude which
is a contrapuntal tour de force. While, to the ear,
the effect is that of a simple and delightful waltz, a
reference to the score (cf. p. 13) reveals a consum-
mate welding of five voices: The GINGERBREAD
WALTZ (25), NASCHWALZER (20), INVITATION
MELODY (22) and the ENTICEMENT (18), the latter
appearing first in the bass and then following, in
canon form, in the Glockenspiel.

The children waltz gaily about and across to the
cottage, where they proceed to take possession of all
the goodies in sight.

There is a loud crackling in the oven; the flames
rise high, and a crash follows as the oven falls to
pieces. Hänsel and Gretel rush to the spot and stand
in silent astonishment, which grows as they become
aware of the row of children near them, whose cake
disguise has magically disappeared.

"We're saved! we're saved!" the children softly
breathe to the accompaniment of a figure derived
from the EVENSONG (2). They beg to be touched
that they may waken into life, and Gretel gently
caresses the nearest child, who smiles and opens its
eyes. Gretel succeeds in wakening the children one
after another, but they remain motionless until Hänsel picks up the juniper branch and sings the COUN-
TERCHARM (24) to the accompaniment of the motive
of DELIVERANCE (26).

So the children are freed from their enchantment
and, joining hands in a circle around Hänsel and
Gretel, they offer their devoted thanks. The motive
of MORNING (19) returns as Hänsel and Gretel,
mindful of their dream come true, give thanks to the
angels who promised all this glory and fulfilled it.
The MORNING SONG (19) and the motive of DE-
LIVERANCE (26) play on, and are only broken into
when from a distance is heard the voice of the Broommaker with his familiar refrain:

"Rallalala, rallalala,

Hungry folk enjoy their meals."

As parents and children see one another, however, and rush to meet, the motive of DELIVERANCE (26) returns and there are the gayest and happiest of greetings.

(26)

Meanwhile the boys have dragged the gingerbread form of the Witch from the ruins of the oven. They all burst into a joyous shout, and the orchestra brings back the gay mood of the first act with a variant of the children's DANCE (3). The Broommaker gives thanks to a gracious Providence for the way a Witch has herself been bewitched and ends with his favourite text:

> "When your need is at its height
> God will set all things aright."

This text is taken up by the children, who sing it in unison to the melody of the EVENSONG (2), accompanied by the full orchestra, giving the effect of a hymn of thanksgiving. But as the keynote of the opera is joy and not solemnity, there is once more a brief return to the mood and motion of the DANCE (3), and so the final curtain falls.

THE END

Titles published by Travis & Emery:

Bathe, William: A Briefe Introduction to the Skill of Song
Bax, Arnold: Symphony #5, Arranged for Piano for Four Hands by Walter Emery
Burney, Charles: An Account of the Musical Performances in Westminster-Abbey
Burney, Charles: The Present State of Music in France and Italy
Burney, Charles: The Present State of Music in Germany, The Netherlands ...
Crimp, Bryan: Solo: The Biography of Solomon
Frescobaldi, Girolamo: D'Arie Musicali per Cantarsi. Primo Libro & Secondo Libro.
Geminiani, Francesco: The Art of Playing the Violin.
Hawkins, John: A General History of the Science and Practice of Music (5 vols.)
Herbert-Caesari, Edgar: The Science and Sensations of Vocal Tone
Herbert-Caesari, Edgar: Vocal Truth
Isaacs, Lewis: Hänsel and Gretel. A Guide to Humperdinck's Opera.
Isaacs, Lewis: Königskinder (Royal Children) A Guide to Humperdinck's Opera.
Lascelles (née Catley), Anne: The Life of Miss Anne Catley.
Mainwaring, John: Memoirs of the Life of the Late George Frederic Handel
Malcolm, Alexander: A Treaty of Music: Speculative, Practical and Historical
Mellers, Wilfrid: Angels of the Night: Popular Female Singers of Our Time
Mellers, Wilfrid: Bach and the Dance of God
Mellers, Wilfrid: Beethoven and the Voice of God
Mellers, Wilfrid: Caliban Reborn - Renewal in Twentieth Century Music
Mellers, Wilfrid: François Couperin and the French Classical Tradition
Mellers, Wilfrid: Harmonious Meeting
Mellers, Wilfrid: Le Jardin Retrouvé, The Music of Frederic Mompou
Mellers, Wilfrid: Music and Society, England and the European Tradition
Mellers, Wilfrid: Music in a New Found Land: ... ... American Music
Mellers, Wilfrid: Romanticism and the Twentieth Century (from 1800)
Mellers, Wilfrid: The Masks of Orpheus: ...... the Story of European Music.
Mellers, Wilfrid: The Sonata Principle (from c. 1750)
Mellers, Wilfrid: Vaughan Williams and the Vision of Albion
Playford, John: An Introduction to the Skill of Musick.
Playford, John: Musick's Recreation on The Viol, Lyra Way. (1682).
Purcell, Henry et al: Harmonia Sacra ... The First Book, [1726]
Purcell, Henry et al: Harmonia Sacra ... Book II [1726]
Rastall, Richard: The Notation of Western Music.
Rubinstein, Anton : Guide to the proper use of the Pianoforte Pedals.
Simpson, Christopher: A Compendium of Practical Musick in Five Parts
Tans'ur, William: A New Musical Grammar; or The Harmonical Spectator
Tosi, Pier Francesco: Observations on the Florid Song.
Van der Straeten, Edmund: History of the Violoncello, The Viol da Gamba ...
Van der Straeten, Edmund: History of the Violin, Its Ancestors... Vol.1.
Van der Straeten, Edmund: History of the Violin, Its Ancestors... Vol.2.

Travis & Emery Music Bookshop
17 Cecil Court, London, WC2N 4EZ, United Kingdom. Tel. (+44) 20 7240 2129
© Travis & Emery 2009

www.ingramcontent.com/pod-product-compliance
Lightning Source LLC
Chambersburg PA
CBHW020448100426
42813CB00026B/2997